D0464114

LEADING
WOMEN

Jeannette Rankin

CORINNE J. NADEN

Cavendish
Square

New York

Published in 2014 by Cavendish Square Publishing, LLC
303 Park Avenue South, Suite 1247, New York, NY 10010

First Edition

Website: cavendishsq.com

This publication represents the opinions and views of the author based on his or her personal experience,
knowledge, and research. The information in this book serves as a general guide only. The author and
publisher have used their best efforts in preparing this book and disclaim liability rising directly or indirectly
from the use and application of this book.

CPSIA Compliance Information: Batch #WS13CSQ

All websites were available and accurate when this book was sent to press.

Library of Congress Cataloging-in-Publication Data
Naden, Corinne J.
Jeanette Rankin / Corinne J. Naden.
p. cm. — (Leading women)
Includes bibliographical references and index.
Summary: "Presents the biography of Jeannette Rankin against the backdrop of her political, historical,
and cultural environment"—Provided by publisher.
ISBN 978-0-7614-4963-8 (hardcover)   ISBN 978-1-62712-118-7 (paperback)
ISBN 978-1-60870-717-1 (ebook)
1. Rankin, Jeannette, 1880-1973. 2. Women legislators—United
States—Biography. 3. Women pacifists—United States—Biography.
4. Suffragists—Montana—Biography. I. Title.
E748.R223N33 2012
328.73'092—dc22 [B]
2010047559

Editor: Deborah Grahame-Smith   Art Director: Anahid Hamparian   Series Designer: Nancy Sabato
Photo research by Connie Gardner

Cover art by Katie Travelstead

The photographs in this book are used by permission and through the courtesy of: *AP Photos*: 1, 32,
75, 76; *Getty Images*: FPG: 4, 48; Herbert, 7; Jacob A Riis, 26' Topical Press Agency, 38; D McAvoy/Time/
Life, 58; Roger Violett, 60; Margaret Bourke White, 71; Hulton Archive, 81; Alex Wong, 84; *Montana
Historical Society*: 11, 14, 17, 20, 34, 42, 55, 72; *Corbis*: Bettmann, 47, 65; Historical, 51.

Printed in the United States of America

CONTENTS

CHAPTER ONE

The World Is Mine

S HE WAS KNOWN AS THE LADY FROM MONTANA, a lifelong fighter for peace and social justice. In a time when American women did not have the right to vote, much less to hold public office, Jeannette Rankin became the first woman elected to the U.S. Congress. She won a seat in the House of Representatives on November 7, 1916. Although women had gained voting rights in Rankin's home state two years earlier, the Nineteenth Amendment, granting women the right to vote in all the states, would not be passed until 1920.

On April 2 of the following year, Jeannette Rankin walked into the great hall in the nation's capitol to take her place in the Sixty-fifth Congress. The clerk of the House of Representatives began the alphabetical roll call. When he reached her name, the congressmen and the visitors in the gallery stood up and cheered. Rankin stood and accepted their recognition with a smile and a slight bow of her head.

Rankin surely made the newspaper headlines in 1916, when those eligible to vote said yes. Twenty-five years later, she was in the headlines again—this time because *she* said no.

The second time was December 8, 1941. The thirty-second president of the United States, Franklin Delano Roosevelt, was speaking to a joint session of Congress. He began, "Yesterday, December seventh, 1941—a date which will live in infamy—the United States of America was suddenly and deliberately attacked by naval and air forces of the Empire of Japan."

Pacifist Jeannette Rankin, first woman elected to the U.S. Congress (1916) and only member who voted no to American entry in both World War I (1917) and World War II (1941)

With these words, Roosevelt was asking Congress to declare war on Japan. Article I of the U.S. Constitution gives Congress the power to declare war. With such a declaration, the United States would enter World War II.

Twenty-one minutes after Roosevelt's speech, the U.S. Senate cast its vote for war, 82 to 0. Then it was up to the House of Representatives. Twelve minutes later, that vote was counted. The House voted 388 to 1. Only one member of Congress said no to war. She was Jeannette Rankin, Republican from Montana.

Why did the first female member of the U.S. Congress go against all of her colleagues? The United States had just been attacked. The American people were angry and afraid. What gave Rankin the courage to stand up for her beliefs even when the entire country seemed to be on the opposite side? And what happened to Rankin as a result of her decision? The answers begin back in Montana, even before it was a state.

THE WILD WEST

Montana is the West, the Great Plains, and the Rocky Mountains. It is also a land of the hearty, the land of the pioneers. And it was the land of Jeannette Rankin in a time when Montana was still a territory. It did not become the forty-first state until Rankin was nine years old, in 1889.

There was lots of space in Montana when young Jeannette was growing up. There still is. Montana stretches more than 147,000 square miles (380,000 square kilometers) across the northwestern United States. Only three states—Alaska, Texas, and California—have more land. And only two states—Alaska and Wyoming—have fewer people. For Jeannette, it was a wonderful place to stretch her legs . . . and her mind.

A typical homestead in the western United States, late nineteenth century

Late-nineteenth-century American society was prejudiced against women in the areas of education, labor laws, voting rights, and land ownership. Discrimination toward women also existed in the West, but women there were more likely to own land, and western states were the first to give the vote to female citizens.

Jeannette Rankin not only came from pioneer land, but also came from pioneer people. New Hampshire, a state in the heart of New England, was not exactly a hotbed of rugged western spirit. But Olive Pickering, Jeannette's mother, must have caught that spirit somehow. At twenty-four years old, she was a single schoolteacher. Teaching was one of the few professions open to women at the time. In fact, the census of 1870 showed that about two-thirds of teachers in the United States were women. To become a teacher was an accomplishment for Pickering and other women of her time. It showed they had received more than a basic education.

Accomplished or not, Olive Pickering was bored. Besides her teaching duties, she found little that interested her, and marriage seemed unlikely at the time. In the late 1800s—and well into the next century—it was typical for women to marry and raise a family rather than pursuing a career outside the home. Olive was not typical.

It was Olive's uncle, Bill, who got her to go west. On the trail of gold, Bill Berry had traveled to California during the Gold Rush in 1849. When gold surfaced in the Montana Territory in the 1860s, he was there, too. Berry even became the sheriff of Missoula, a Montana town. He sent home stories about gold miners, cowboys, and eligible bachelors. His letter about an opening for a schoolteacher in Missoula sounded exciting—at least to Olive.

But what self-respecting New Hampshire parents would let their young, unmarried daughter take a journey into the Wild West? Apparently, Olive's mother and father were up for it. With the promise that Olive's sister, Mandanna (Mannie), would go along, the Pickerings said yes to the journey. (Even though she was engaged at the time, Mandanna agreed to the plan; she returned home in a few months.)

So, Olive and her sister ventured west in 1878. It was a bumpy—and very long—ride. First, there was the train, which sped along at 30 miles (48 kilometers) an hour. Then came the stage, a four-wheeled, horse-drawn coach that ran from Corinne, Utah, to Butte City over a rough and dangerous trail. From Butte City, the trip was about 130 miles (210 km) to Missoula. Robbery was practically a sport along this stretch of the stage journey, but Olive and Mannie got through unharmed.

THE PICKERINGS' CLAIM TO FAME

Jeannette Rankin could trace her ancestry to Revolutionary War officer Timothy Pickering (1845–1829) of Salem, Massachusetts. During the Revolutionary War, Pickering served as quartermaster general under George Washington. After the war he became Indian commissioner and postmaster general. From 1795 to 1800, he had the distinction of serving in the first two U.S. presidential cabinets. Pickering was secretary of state under both George Washington and John Adams, but he was dismissed after a policy dispute with Adams.

Rankin also might have traced her antiwar sentiments back to Pickering. As a senator from Massachusetts (1803–1811) and then a congressman (1813–1817), Pickering was bitterly opposed to the War of 1812. The Treaty of Ghent, signed in 1814, ended this war between England and the United States.

In this way, Olive Pickering arrived in Montana to take up her teaching position. But her career in Missoula hardly seemed longer than the journey. By the end of the year, the call went out for a new teacher to replace her. It wasn't that Olive didn't like her teaching job in Missoula. The bustling town was slightly younger than she was and already had a population of more than three hundred. Besides the school, it boasted a Methodist church, a bank, and two stores. Actually, teaching in Missoula didn't seem much different from teaching back in New Hampshire.

WOMEN IN THE WEST

America's frontier moved steadily west during the 1800s. By the latter part of the century, the West was a patchwork of farms, ranches, small towns, and growing cities. Women in the West tended the homes and vegetable gardens and taught the children. They became tailors and dressmakers. Although American women in general faced discrimination throughout the country, western states were the first to approach more equal treatment between the sexes. The Wyoming Territory was the first to pass a law giving women the vote in 1869. Utah followed suit the following year, but the U.S. Congress vetoed that law. In 1890, Wyoming became the first U.S. state giving women the vote; Colorado became the second state three years later. Utah tried again in 1895, when the state adopted a constitution that restored wo-men's suffrage. Idaho followed the next year.

What happened to Olive Pickering in Missoula—and caused her to quit teaching—was what hadn't happened in New Hampshire. She fell in love.

CHILDHOOD IN MONTANA

Olive fell in love with John Rankin, a thirty-eight-year-old Scotch Canadian with red hair. He was truly the pioneer of what became Jeannette's family. Rankin had limited education but great skill as a carpenter. He and a brother had traveled much of Montana and the

Missouri River. When he met Olive Pickering at a barn dance, John was running a successful lumber business. He was almost blind in one eye due to a cannon blast. Although John was said to be a quiet man, rumor had it that he could dance a lively jig when motivated.

After John and Olive married in 1879, they moved into a ranch house in Grant Greek, outside Missoula. The couple planned to raise chickens, vegetables, and children. Jeannette, the first of the Rankin clan, was born on June 11, 1880. After Jeannette came Philena (who died in early childhood), Harriet, Wellington, Mary, and, after a spell of a few years, Grace, followed by Edna.

It was an exciting time to grow up in America and in Montana. The western territory was young, rough, and expanding. Towns, schools, businesses, and churches were sprouting everywhere. There was a feeling that if you worked hard, the world was yours. And that's

The Rankin clan: (*l. to r., front row*) John, Mary, Edna, Grace, Wellington, Olive; (*back row*) Jeannette, Harriet, and a photograph of Philena, who died in childhood

INFANT MORTALITY

The Rankins' second child, Philena, died at an early age. This was not rare in the late nineteenth century, when most children were born at home with midwives in attendance. At that time, the childbirth mortality rate was slightly more than 150 per 1,000 births. Toward the beginning of the twentieth century, hospital births became increasingly popular. Today, the U.S. infant mortality rate is a little more than six deaths out of every thousand births. According to the CIA World Factbook data from 2010, that compares with 2.31 deaths for every 1,000 births in Singapore and more than 180 deaths per 1,000 births in Angola.

how Jeannette grew up—with the feeling that the world was indeed hers. She was strong-minded and—according to her mother—a handful. In fact, Olive once said to her husband: "If you can take care of Jeannette, I can take care of the rest of the children." However, she did help her father with all the chores that might have been expected of the oldest son. When Wellington, the only boy in the family, was in his teens, he took responsibility for handling his father's business records. But everyone, regardless of gender and age, had responsibilities in the Rankin camp.

Young Jeannette could be harsh and demanding, and she often disregarded others' opinions. But when she saw people in pain, she tried to do something about it. A well-known story from her childhood involves a badly cut horse on the Rankin ranch. Jeannette's father called for her to sew up the wound, and she calmly tended to the horse with needle and thread.

Jeannette could also use hammer and nails when necessary. And as the oldest girl in the family, she had responsibilities in the home. These largely involved taking charge of the younger children, which she did with a no-nonsense air of authority.

GETTING AN EDUCATION

When Jeannette was five years old and ready for school, the family began spending only summers on the ranch. They moved to Missoula and into a ten-room house that John built. Its bathtub and running water made it one of the finest homes in the area. There was plenty to do in the growing city of Missoula. The lakes froze in winter for ice-skating, there was Saturday night barn dancing, and friends visited for Sunday night suppers. But Jeannette still liked summers on the ranch best. Although she was intelligent, she was not a particularly good student. There was always something better to do than study a book. She relished the freedom of the outdoors. When she could get out of her household chores, she rode on horseback with her father as he worked with the ranch hands.

The Rankins did not emphasize religion with their children. Jeannette and her siblings went to the Presbyterian Church Sunday school, but her parents rarely attended services. Jeannette later said that there was little discipline in the family. They often solved disputes by shouting or throwing things.

Some sources say that Jeannette once thought of becoming a nurse, but her father discouraged her. Supposedly he claimed she wasn't healthy enough. There is no record, however, of illness or physical problems throughout Jeannette's adult years.

The Rankins' newly finished house in Missoula, Montana

In the 1890s, few families in the state of Montana had the luxuries that the Rankins enjoyed. In fact, the Rankins lived more luxuriously than *most* Americans. Life was hard at that time. Many people, including children, worked twelve or more hours a day, six days a week, in factories or mines. Survival was the key issue; school was often forgotten in the struggle. But the Rankins, perhaps due to Olive's background, were determined to educate their children. The Rankin kids all attended school in Missoula, and Jeannette graduated from high school in 1898.

In the late nineteenth century, American teenagers generally were not expected to go to college. In fact, only about 2 percent of young Americans graduated from high school in 1900. However, all the Rankin girls went to Montana State University. By the time Jeannette enrolled, the school was three years old. The faculty numbered thirteen, and Missoula's population had grown to five thousand.

If Jeannette was impressed with herself for attending college, she didn't show it. In fact, she wasn't really interested in attending school at all. She was more or less just passing the time until something really caught her attention. One of her teachers later remembered her in this way: "She was an extremely timid girl and worked hard for what she got." However, her sisters, when their turns came, were apparently more impressed with the college. Harriet would become the dean of women at Montana State, Mary taught English there, and Edna was the first woman to earn a law degree from the school.

Jeannette's brother, Wellington, was the only Rankin child who did not attend Montana State. He was sent east to Harvard University. Established in 1636 in Cambridge, Massachusetts, Harvard is among the most prestigious of U.S. colleges. Wellington was handsome, opinionated, sure of himself, and an eloquent speaker. Later he would graduate from Harvard Law School and return to Montana, where he became a wealthy businessman.

Jeannette and her brother had always been rivals. Intelligent and strong-willed, they vied for family attention throughout their childhood. However, it did not seem to bother Jeannette that Wellington went to a more impressive university. Jeannette never showed anything but affection for Wellington, although she long remained in his shadow. In fact, all the Rankin girls remained in his shadow. To a large extent, Wellington directed their lives. He sent them money, prepared their taxes, saw to the education of their own children, and gave them advice.

It seemed Wellington always got what he wanted. On one occasion in 1942, he called for Jeannette to come home immediately to take care of their mother for a short period. By then Jeannette was in Congress, but she obeyed even though it was a busy week in Washington.

Wellington tried his hand at politics, too, but in this he failed. He ran for office seven times and was elected just once, in 1920, as state attorney general. He did, however, succeed in building one of the largest ranching empires in the country. Upon his death, it was valued at $9 million.

Despite her determined nature, Jeannette Rankin, unlike her brother, never turned into a serious student. In fact, she later complained that college had taught her not to think. Her major course of study was biology, and she wrote a senior thesis about snail shells. She enjoyed collecting and weighing snail parts, but she did not like writing the thesis itself. One of eighteen in her class, Jeannette graduated from Montana State in 1902.

WHAT TO DO NOW?

By now Jeannette Rankin was a young woman of medium height with reddish hair, gray-blue eyes, a long nose, and a wide mouth. She made her own clothes. The style of the day was a long, wool skirt with a white cotton blouse called a shirtwaist, which had puffy sleeves known as leg-of-mutton, and a wide belt.

Quiet and reserved in school, Jeannette nonetheless had many friends. After graduation, she and two other girls from school took a train to the West Coast. After they returned, she spent the rest of the summer helping to care for her younger siblings. She also attended showers and wedding receptions for her friends. There was no hint of a wedding reception for Jeannette, however; she said later that

Rankin doing snail research at the University of Washington

taking care of her siblings left her little time for anything else. And as yet there was no hint of an interest in politics, although she was concerned about voting rights for women. As she said in her essay "Two Votes Against War: 1917 and 1941,"

"
I had been deeply involved in the preceding years in the struggle for woman suffrage. That struggle and the struggle against war were integrally related in my youthful thoughts and activities.
"

LAND-GRANT UNIVERSITIES

Jeannette and her sisters attended Montana State University, which became the University of Montana in 1965. This school is a so-called land-grant university, one of many designated by U.S. states to receive benefits of the Morrill Acts of 1862 and 1890. The Morrill Acts granted federally controlled land to individual states to establish land-grant colleges that focused on agriculture, science, and engineering. The first such institution was Michigan State University, designated in 1855 as the Agricultural College of the State of Michigan. The oldest school with land-grant status is Rutgers University, the state college of New Jersey, founded in 1766 and designated in 1864. Land-grant schools were typical in the early West and drew large numbers of female students.

Some say that the pacifism that would later become part of Rankin's philosophy stemmed from the fact that her father did not carry a gun. Contrary to popular opinion, however, many westerners did not carry guns during that period. Much later Rankin recalled, "Deep down, I guess I had always felt strongly about war." At the time of her college graduation, the United States had recently won the Spanish-American War (1898), which ended Spanish colonial rule in the Americas.

But what was Jeannette to do with her future? Like many educated young women of the time, she decided to become a teacher. She taught first at Grant Creek and then about 150 miles (240 km) from Missoula. Still dissatisfied, she returned home and worked in a department store. Missoula now had a population of about eight thousand.

Besides her indecision, other events combined to keep Jeannette at home. In 1904, two years after her graduation from Montana State, her father died after contracting Rocky Mountain spotted fever—a potentially fatal illness even today. Jeannette had little choice but to help her mother take care of the family. Wellington, then nineteen, came home to set the ranch's finances in order. As for Olive, she had given most of the family responsibilities to Jeannette by this time.

Jeannette had little time to think about a career. Some sources say that her younger siblings objected to her overbearing authority. But, like it or not, Jeannette Rankin now ran the family.

CHAPTER TWO

The Turning Point

F OR THE NEXT FOUR YEARS, JEANNETTE RANKIN shouldered the responsibilities of caring for her family. Wellington was a more than competent financial manager. Leaving the ranch's accounts in good shape, he returned to Harvard. Jeannette did not have to worry about money; her allowance of seventy-five dollars a month took care of her needs.

But Jeannette remained restless. She did not know what she wanted to do. So, when Wellington hinted that he was ill, Jeannette pledged to take care of him. After persuading a friend, Jimmie Mills, to go with her, she left her mother and siblings for a six-month trip to the East Coast.

These six months were a marvelous vacation for the young women. Wellington speedily recovered from his illness and showed Jeannette and Jimmie the sights of Boston. Then they traveled to Washington, D.C., for the 1905 inauguration of Theodore Roosevelt. A congressman from Missoula got them tickets to the president's inaugural ball. Wellington, a progressive Republican, was impressed with Roosevelt. Jeannette and Jimmie also traveled to New York City and stayed at the elegant Waldorf Astoria Hotel, thanks to Jimmie's brother, a Missoula doctor who was visiting the city.

THE GERM OF AN IDEA

Jeannette returned to Montana. Now only her mother and her two youngest sisters, Grace and Edna, were living at home.

Rankin and brother, Wellington, in front of the family home in Missoula, about 1914

Jeannette's mind was filled with contrasting impressions of her six-month journey. She had walked along the famed Fifth Avenue in New York City. She had looked into shop windows at luxurious clothes. She had admired the wealthy people as they rode by in their fine carriages. But she had also seen the slum neighborhoods of New York, Boston, and the nation's capital. It had been a quick glance into how a good many Americans lived. Compared to her relatively comfortable life in Missoula, the poverty in these places was a shock to Jeannette.

With these pictures of misery firmly in her mind, Jeannette returned to her family duties and took up some serious reading. She bought a copy of *The Long Day: The Story of a New York Working Girl as Told by Herself* (1906). This book would remain on her library shelf all her life. She also became interested in the writings of Jane Addams, a pacifist and social reformer.

Still searching for something meaningful to do, Rankin visited an aunt and uncle in San Francisco in 1907. The city had not totally recovered from the great fire and earthquake that had hit the previous year. She decided to take a job at a settlement house in San Francisco's Telegraph Hill neighborhood. Settlement homes were an approach to social reform by having social workers live with the poor people they were trying to serve. As residents, it was felt that the workers would find more effective ways of dealing with the problems of the urban poor.

Today, Telegraph Hill is one of San Francisco's desirable areas. It is a maze of impossibly crooked streets and hidden gardens looking down from a lofty height over San Francisco Bay. But back in 1907, Telegraph Hill consisted of crowded living space for largely Italian and poor immigrants. The neighborhood's residents spoke little English, held only the lowest-paying jobs, had little access to health care, and faced almost constant discrimination.

JANE ADDAMS

Jane Addams (1860–1935) was born in Illinois. She was the eighth of nine children. Addams graduated from the Rockford Female Seminary in 1881, but ill health forced her to discontinue medical studies.

After visiting the Toynbee Hall settlement house in London, Addams created Hull House, the first social settlement in North America, in 1889. Hull House began in a working-class district of Chicago. Eventually, the settlement grew to include thirteen buildings, a playground, and a camp near Geneva, Wisconsin. It provided services and cultural opportunities for the area's largely immigrant population. Hull House was also a place for social workers to train.

Addams worked all her life for justice for immigrants and for women's right to vote. She suffered from ill health for many years. In December 1931, on the day she was admitted to a Baltimore hospital, Addams learned she had won the Nobel Peace Prize.

EARTHQUAKE ROCKS SAN FRANCISCO

On Wednesday morning, April 18, 1906, at 5:12 a.m., a major earthquake hit San Francisco and the northern California coast. Caused by a rupture in the San Andreas Fault, this quake was one of the worst natural disasters in American history. The shaking that resulted from the main shock lasted some forty seconds. But as damaging as the quake and its aftershocks were, the fire that followed was worse. It destroyed more than five hundred blocks of the downtown area. More than three thousand people died as a result of the quake and the fire.

While working on Telegraph Hill, Rankin began to find herself. She taught English and hygiene to the children. She attended meetings on child labor laws and working conditions for the poor. She watched how the social workers tried to ease the misery of these people. And finally, she knew where she belonged. In 1908, now twenty-eight years old, she went back to New York City. This time she was not on vacation. She was going to become a social worker.

As a profession, social work originated mainly in the United States and England in the late nineteenth century. It involves social change and the pursuit of social welfare. Social workers are dedicated to improving the quality of life and the development of individuals and groups within society. When the field emerged, there were no federal or state agencies to do this work, and women stepped in almost exclusively. Today, both men and women are social workers. Among the field's best-known practitioners, in addition to Jane Addams and Jeannette Rankin, are Frances Perkins, the first woman cabinet member (she was Franklin D. Roosevelt's secretary of labor from 1933 to 1945), and civil rights trailblazer Whitney M. Young Jr.

BACK TO SCHOOL

The Summer School in Philanthropic Work opened in New York City in 1898. It was the first national higher-education program to train social workers. In 1904, the school's name changed to the New York School of Philanthropy. By the time Rankin arrived, the course had been expanded to full-time graduate study. (In 1917, it became the New York School of Social Work, and in 1963, it was renamed the Columbia University School of Social Work.)

Rankin's program consisted of morning lectures and hands-on work in the afternoons. She spent time in the lower Manhattan district known as the Bowery. Once the center of theater life in New York, the Bowery had deteriorated in the 1880s. Home to derelicts and others down on their luck, it had become a skid-row area of cheap flophouses, saloons, and pawnshops. She also spent time in night court, where she tried to help young girls escape prostitution. She helped find schools and health services for deaf children. As Rankin traveled the slums of the city, she was often shocked by the poverty that she had not seen in the relatively young settled lands of the West.

These people in need made a lasting and deep impression on Jeannette Rankin, as did the school itself. During her studies there in 1908 and 1909, the faculty was composed mainly of women. The

THE SLUMS OF NEW YORK

In New York City, as in other American cities in the late 1800s, people were often crowded into tenements known as slum areas. Many of the buildings in New York were already more than a century old. Massive immigration was swelling the city's population. Poor and unemployed people—many of whom were immigrants who had come to the United States to find the "American dream"—lived in small, dark rooms where they ate and slept, often with no heat and sharing one toilet to a floor. Hoping for better lives for their children, they found work where and when they could. There was rarely enough food for everyone, and it was often necessary for children to go to work to earn money instead of going to school.

Immigrants such as this woman and her baby often endured deplorable conditions in the tenements of New York City in the late 1800s.

student body, which included students from foreign countries as well as the United States, was mostly female as well. These were intelligent and determined people dedicated to a cause. Rankin felt challenged, almost awed, by the women around her. They taught her to think about life's values in a completely new way. She had always been strong-willed and determined, but now she found a channel for her feelings.

Rankin graduated from the New York School of Philanthropy in spring 1909. She returned to Missoula and decided that her first social work project would be to investigate the county jail. She lectured about the jail's rotten food and deplorable sanitary conditions. She argued that prostitutes should not be housed in the same cells with male offenders. The local officials either ignored her or laughed.

Rankin moved on to Spokane, Washington, to an orphanage called the Washington Children's Home Society. Here, at least, she could help the children. But once again she felt frustrated by the workers' seeming lack of initiative. Or perhaps, she speculated, it was just that the social workers did not have the right answers to the problems they confronted. Perhaps they did not have the right tools—or the right laws—to correct terrible social conditions.

Looking for answers, Rankin spent a year studying economics and sociology at the University of Washington. She no longer had a job, but she was still receiving seventy-five dollars a month from the ranch, and she made extra money by sewing for a dressmaker. These sources of income allowed her to work for free. For example, if the university needed someone to put up posters about children's services in poor neighborhoods, Rankin was the first to raise her hand. A colleague later said there was no job too difficult for her if it meant improving social services for the poor.

When Rankin left the university, she not only felt better prepared in her chosen work, but also was ready to take on a new cause. It was 1910, and a movement was afoot. It concerned a somewhat novel concept: women should have the right to vote.

WOMEN'S SUFFRAGE

Suffrage is the right to vote. Once upon a time in the world, women could not vote for the politicians and laws that ruled their lives. In some nations women still can't vote, although the list is growing shorter.

The first major modern nation to grant women's suffrage was New Zealand, in 1893. It took twenty-seven more years for women to gain that right in the United States. Those years were long and difficult. Much of the credit for the outcome goes to the work of activists such as Jeannette Rankin.

American women began to call for voting rights in the early nineteenth century, when the country was beginning to boil over slavery. Lucretia Mott and Elizabeth Cady Stanton held an antislavery convention in Seneca Falls, New York, in July 1848. In 1852, Stanton and suffragist leader Susan B. Anthony joined forces in Syracuse, New York, and led the movement for the next fifty years.

At first, these women and their supporters tried to win the vote through amendments to state constitutions. But by 1869, after the Civil War, only the Territory of Wyoming allowed women's suffrage. It was increasingly obvious that nothing short of an amendment to the U.S. Constitution was going to give American women the right to vote. Toward that end, the National Woman Suffrage Association was formed in 1869. Lucy Stone later established the American Woman Suffrage Association. The two groups joined forces to become the National American Woman Suffrage Association in 1890. That was also the year Wyoming entered the Union. Its state constitution was

THEY WERE A FORCE

Lucretia Mott (1793–1880), a native of Massachusetts, became interested in the women's movement while working as a schoolteacher. She was paid only half the salary that her male colleagues were receiving. After joining forces with Elizabeth Stanton, Mott spent her time lecturing and fighting for the right to vote. When she died at age eighty-seven, she was regarded as one of the most effective reformers in the country.

New York–born Elizabeth Cady Stanton (1815–1902) studied law in the office of her father, who later became a New York State Supreme Court judge. Working with Mott, she drew up resolutions that demanded improvements to the status of women, including the right to vote.

Susan Brownell Anthony (1820–1906) was a crusader whose work opened the door for passage of the Nineteenth Amendment. She was tireless in her quest to end slavery and to give women the right to vote. With Stanton and Matilda Gage, she published *The History of Woman Suffrage* (4 volumes, 1881–1902).

the first to give women the right to vote, although other states had already granted local voting rights to women.

But now it was 1910, and voters in the state of Washington were preparing to decide on suffrage for women. Rankin was determined to help the cause. She organized meetings, put up posters, and talked to anyone who would listen. And when the results were tallied—and women in the state of Washington gained the right to vote—Rankin felt she had played a small part in the victory.

But the fight had just begun. Washington was only the fifth state—following Wyoming, Utah, Colorado, and Idaho—in which female citizens of the United States of America could vote. Rankin had come this far; there was no turning back. If it worked in Washington, why not try in Montana?

Rankin returned to Missoula in December. In February she delivered a speech to the state legislature. By now she had become a forceful speaker—quiet, dignified, and convincing. There were many reasons, she explained, why women should have the right to vote. For one, they had worked side by side with their husbands and brothers to build the land and to carry Montana to statehood.

Rankin's reasons were all true, but they fell on largely deaf ears. Practically everyone in the state now knew who Jeannette Rankin was. But Montana remained on the men-only-voters list.

It was time to take the next step: if Rankin couldn't take on Montana, she would take on the whole country. Harriet Laidlaw, head of the Woman Suffrage Party, offered her fifty dollars a month to work for her in New York City. In spring 1911, Rankin was back on the eastbound train.

Laidlaw put Rankin to work promoting the cause of women's votes on city street corners. She gathered names and opinions on women's suffrage and spoke to anyone who walked by. Lots of people ignored her or thought she was a lunatic, but many listened as well. She was a good speaker who grew even more forceful as she became more confident and dedicated to the cause.

Laidlaw soon recognized Rankin's talent and decided that she could be an important front-runner on the suffrage issue. First, she sent Rankin to California, where she worked to get out the message in San Francisco and surrounding areas. She returned to lead a women's suffrage lobbying effort at the legislature in Albany, the capital of New York State. In Canton, Ohio, she handed out pamphlets at factory gates. Over the next months, it seemed that Jeannette Rankin was all over the country. She traveled thousands of miles and made hundreds of speeches.

Upon his inauguration in March 1912, Woodrow Wilson became the first Democratic party president in two decades. Suffragists organized a march to demand the vote, and about five thousand people showed up. The police had underestimated the number of officers it would take to control the crowd. At various points, people spit upon the marchers, pelted them with cigar butts, and threw them to the ground. For women like Jeannette Rankin and other advocates of women's right to vote, equality seemed a long way off.

By 1914, women had gained the right to vote in just ten of forty-eight states. (Arizona and New Mexico gained statehood in 1912.) Montana was not one of the ten. Rankin decided to go home and carry on the fight there. Some of her coworkers from New York joined her. Together, they traveled the state and spread the message in cities, towns, and ranches. Covering over 5,000 miles (8,000 km) in five months, they talked at schools, in union halls, and on street corners. In order to succeed, the suffragists had to get their message across to the foreign-born population, which was now up to about 20 percent. In one sense, they also had to fight the powerful Anaconda Copper

Company, which owned most of the state's major newspapers. It was difficult to publicize the suffrage campaign because Anaconda's leaders were not in favor of women's suffrage and, therefore, the newspapers tended to ignore the issue. But the women's message, wherever they could voice it, was always the same: American women

Suffragists from New York march to the Woman Suffrage Procession in Washington, D.C., on the eve of Woodrow Wilson's inauguration, March 1913.

JEANNETTE RANKIN

must have the right to vote. Any citizen, regardless of gender, should have the right to vote.

Not everyone thought so. Many men and some women of the time were against suffrage. In 1911, J. B. Sanford, chairman of the Democratic caucus, argued that since suffrage is a privilege and not a right

and politics is no place for a woman, the privilege should not be granted to her. Despite the cries of such groups, Rankin and her coworkers made an impression. On November 3, 1914, the men of Montana approved a woman's right to vote by a margin of just four points.

It was a good fight, but it was not over. Eleven states now granted full voting rights. Yet, there could be no victory until a constitutional amendment was passed. For that, Rankin and other suffragists would have to wait a few more years.

CHAPTER THREE

A Woman in the House

S OMETIMES A GOOD IDEA TURNS INTO REALITY. That is what happened to the women's suffrage movement. Sometimes a good idea takes a person to a somewhat shocking next step. That is what happened to Jeannette Rankin.

Who knows when the idea came to her? After all, she had been involved in politics for years. She knew how to convince people to take up a cause. She had experienced the rough-and-tumble world that makes up different levels of government in the United States. Or maybe it was just her belief that, as she said later, "We're half the people; we should be half the Congress."

Whatever the reasons behind it, one day in 1915, Jeannette Rankin told a shocked group of female friends that she was planning to run for Congress. She was a bit dismayed at their reactions, which ranged from "You can't win" to "Why don't you try for a lower office?" Apparently it was not going to be easy to convince the voters of Montana to send the first woman to Congress. But by now, Rankin knew that nothing in politics was easy. So, she went to work.

IT'S ABOUT TIME . . .

Jeannette Rankin was now thirty-five years old. She had fought hard in the battle for women's suffrage. But the fight for the vote was nothing compared to what she now faced. A woman in

In 1915 Rankin decided to run for Congress.

the House? "The very audacity," said some. "Government is no place for a woman!" She had heard it all before. Just as she had worked tirelessly for the right to vote, she took on this new challenge with great determination.

First, Rankin enlisted her brother Wellington to be her campaign manager. The rest of the family clan supported her, too. Her sisters and their families traveled all over Montana to show their support. She made speech after speech. She told the women she would fight for child labor laws. She told the men she would fight for better working conditions in the mines and factories. And she told all the people of Montana that she would fight against fighting. Americans throughout the land were getting concerned about the war that was raging in Europe. Would the United States get involved? Rankin vowed she would fight to keep the country out of the madness.

Rankin said later that during her congressional campaign, she used tactics that had worked when trying to get the vote for women. She hired brass bands and held street parades. She organized open-air meetings. She got her family and other supporters to make telephone calls all over the state. Not everyone had a telephone in those days, but anyone who did received a call on election morning: get out and vote for Rankin!

An energetic campaigner, she was happiest when she was on the move. And she persisted with her message. She ignored the hecklers and the naysayers and just kept on talking. Perhaps, finally, the people of Montana decided that the best way to get rid of her was just to listen to her. And, little by little, they began to listen and to believe.

In July 1916, the Good Government League nominated Jeannette Rankin as a candidate for the U.S. Congress. The Good Government League was a national organization created for woman's suffrage. Soon afterward, Rankin announced that she would run on the

Republican ticket for one of the two House seats from Montana. Although Republicans were the minority party in the state, her father had been a Republican, and Wellington was a very powerful Republican businessman in Montana. Once again, as she campaigned all over the state, she fought the hecklers and others who believed a woman's place was definitely not in the House.

And enough people got the message. In November 1916, the ballots were counted. This was a long process, as there were no electronic voting machines. But finally the tally was in.

The Democratic incumbent in Montana took one of the House seats with 84,499 votes. Rankin took the second House seat by beating out the other Republican hopeful, 76,932 votes to 66,974. At first no one seemed willing to believe it. Newspaper editors in the state took their time before they published the story of her victory. Outside the state, people were just astonished. A woman in Congress? One man wrote a letter to the *New York Times* complaining that Rankin's election was plainly illegal. After all, the word *she* was not used in the Constitution!

But, in this case, votes were votes. Shocking or not, it no longer mattered. Jeannette Rankin had just become the first woman to be elected to the United States Congress.

Rankin was a brand-new celebrity. She became the darling of the newspapers, and several organizations invited her to speak. But if the public—still in some shock that a woman had actually been elected to Congress—expected to meet some kind of cowgirl on a western pony, they were disappointed. The new House member was well spoken, well educated, well dressed, well traveled, and at home in the halls of Congress.

After her election, Rankin went on a month-long speaking tour. She arrived in Washington, D.C., on April 1, 1917, and moved into

A crowd watches as Rankin is driven to her swearing in as the first female member of the U.S. Congress, 1917.

a large apartment that she rented for herself and her mother. The following day she had breakfast with a group of suffragists at the Shoreham Hotel. Later that day, dressed in a dark blue silk suit, she walked into the great hall of the nation's capitol to take her place as a member of the Sixty-fifth Congress. With a nod and a smile, she changed U.S. history.

Rankin had just won the fight of her life. But there was little time to sit back and enjoy her hard-won position. Her country was facing a frightening and serious problem.

WOMEN IN CONGRESS

Jeannette Rankin was the first woman elected to the House of Representatives. The first woman to serve in the U.S. Senate was Rebecca Latimer Felton of Georgia. In 1922, mainly in recognition of years of government service, she was appointed to fill a vacancy. The eighty-seven-year-old served just twenty-four hours before a regular election was held for a new senator.

The first woman actually elected to the Senate was Hattie Wyatt Caraway of Arkansas, who took office in 1931. Like many other women who followed her, she was appointed to fill a seat left by her husband's death. She won reelection on her own in 1932. The first woman to win a Senate seat unconnected to her husband was Margaret Chase Smith, Republican of Maine, in 1949. Smith was the first woman to serve in both houses of Congress: the House of Representatives from 1940 to 1949 and the Senate from 1949 to 1973. She was also the first woman to be nominated for the U.S. presidency. This happened in 1964, when Barry Goldwater eventually became the Republican nominee and lost the election to Lyndon Johnson.

THE WAR TO END ALL WARS

Historians cite many causes for World War I, which is often called the Great War or the War to End All Wars. The war began in August 1914. Trouble had been brewing in Europe for some time. By 1910, the major European nations had formed two potentially hostile alliances: France, Great Britain, and Russia on one side, and Germany and Austria on the other. Militarism, which stresses the importance of the military in government, was on the rise. Britain and Germany were competing for mastery of the seas. France and Germany had nearly doubled their armies since the late 1800s. A fierce sense of nationalism—strong loyalty to one's own country—was growing. The European powers were having diplomatic clashes over their colonies.

All this bubbling frustration needed only a spark to bring on war. That spark flew on the morning of June 28, 1914. Archduke Franz Ferdinand, heir to the throne of Austria-Hungary, was in Sarajevo, the capital of Bosnia and Herzegovina. As he and his wife rode in their open car, a man named Gavrilo Princip assassinated them. Suddenly, all the tensions between the European nations formed around a specific rallying cry, and World War I began.

By the end of July 1914, most of Europe was at war. On one side were the Entente—mainly the United Kingdom, France, and Russia, joined by Italy the following year. (An *entente*, from the French, is an agreement between nations for a specific purpose.) The Entente lined up against the Central Powers (Germany and Austria-Hungary), so-called because of their central location in Europe. Later in 1914, the Ottoman Empire joined the Central Powers; Bulgaria followed in 1915.

The war raged along several fronts across the continent—with no involvement from the United States. President Woodrow Wilson followed the traditional American policy of isolationism. That meant not going to war unless American soil was in danger. It also meant not getting dragged into war because of an alliance with another nation. Although the U.S. government did try to bring peace diplomatically, Wilson simply wanted the country to steer clear of Europe's problems. In 1915, however, a German U-boat sank the passenger liner *Lusitania* with 128 Americans aboard. Wilson demanded an end to such attacks, and the Germans seemed to agree. Then, in January 1917, Germany resumed unrestricted submarine warfare. In addition, the British broke a German code and uncovered the Zimmerman Telegram. This was a message urging Mexico to declare war against the United States. This move, the Germans hoped, would prevent the Americans from joining the fight in Europe.

After the Zimmerman Telegram was published and the Germans sank seven U.S. merchant ships, Wilson abandoned isolationism. On the evening of April 2, the opening of the new Congress, he called the Senate and the House of Representatives into a joint session. Wilson asked Congress for a declaration of war against Germany and its allies. Possibly forgetting that the gender makeup of Congress had changed, Wilson said, "It is a distressing oppressive duty, gentlemen of the Congress, which I have performed in thus addressing you. There are, it may be, many months of fiery trial and sacrifice ahead of us. It is a fearful thing to lead a great people into war."

The Senate voted on April 4; eighty-two members voted yes to war, and six said no. The House of Representatives vote was scheduled for April 5.

The new member of Congress thought very long and hard about her decision. And Jeannette Rankin was not without advice. Most leaders of the suffragette cause wanted her to vote for war. They feared a no vote from the first female member of Congress would make women seem irresponsible or too sentimental. Rankin understood their fears.

Rankin at work in her congressional office

But for years, Rankin's hatred of war had been growing. When she was in college, she had read "The Charge of the Light Brigade" by Alfred Lord Tennyson (1809-1892). This poem speaks of the suicidal attack of six hundred soldiers who had no choice " . . . but to do or die." She had called the poem ridiculous and had declared that she couldn't read it. Now she was faced with a real-life choice about war and her convictions. Her congressional career had just begun, and this vote might put it in jeopardy. Harriet Laidlaw made a trip to Washington to convince Rankin to vote for war. Fearful that a no vote would destroy his sister's career, Wellington also traveled to Washington to try to persuade her to vote yes.

It was a very difficult time for Rankin. Wellington's approval meant a good deal to her, as did the opinions of the women she had worked with. Many suffragettes felt that a no vote would undermine much of the work they had done. Rankin thought long and hard about the people who had helped her. She thought about her family. She thought about the new, exciting, and important career that was just starting. But she also thought about all the people who were dying in a terrible war across the Atlantic.

In the end, Jeannette Rankin could only vote her conscience. She knew no other way. She felt she must make a protest against war for all the women of the future. When the time came and the clerk called her name, she rose and spoke in a clear and quiet voice.

I want to stand by my country, but I cannot vote for war. I vote no!

When the roll call was done, 373 members of the House voted for war, 9 did not vote, and 50 members said no. On April 6, 1917, the United States entered World War I.

THE REST OF THE TERM

Six senators and fifty representatives had voted against the war. But to the newspapers and a large part of the American population, it made no difference. Jeannette Rankin was the lone woman in Congress, and she had voted no. Ignoring the men who had done the same, some critics claimed that her negative vote indicated women were not up to the rigors of office. Besides, insisted some of the press, she had cried while casting her vote—something only a woman would do.

Rankin's term as the first woman in Congress had just begun, but she knew it was over. She would not be reelected. However, she did have almost two years left to get something done in Washington. She decided to make good use of that time.

Once the United States was engaged in fighting the war, Rankin did vote to allocate money for troops. However, she voted against the Espionage Act, which mandated a prison term for anyone who interfered with troop recruitment. She also championed the plight of women employees of the U.S. Bureau of Engraving and Printing. Their bosses were forcing them to work twelve to fifteen hours a day in violation of the federal eight-hour law. The bureau's leaders wanted to speed up the production of Liberty Loan bonds, which were sold to promote the cause of World War I. Rankin hired a private detective to investigate working conditions. Then she threatened the bureau's head with a congressional investigation if he did not restore the eight-hour workday. He did.

Rankin worked to establish medical clinics for poor children in rural areas and care centers for the children of factory workers. Whenever possible, she introduced legislation aimed at protecting women and children. Two of her proposed bills called for equal pay for men and women in the same job. She was often unsuccessful in her quest for equal rights and equal pay. One of her achievements, however, was introducing the Rankin-Robinson Bill (with coauthor Senator Joseph Robinson). It provided federal funds for improving rural health education and increased funding for the Children's Bureau, established in 1912 to improve the welfare of the nation's children. Although the bill was held up in the House Labor Committee for a long time, it finally passed in 1921 as the Sheppard-Towner Bill.

Rankin returned to Montana in June. Some 14,000 miners in the city of Butte had gone on strike after losing 260 men in the Speculator Mine. In its heyday, from the late nineteenth century until about 1920, Butte was one of the largest and richest copper boomtowns in the West. Its active labor union had tried to fight the Anaconda Mining Company, known simply as "the company."

On June 8, 1917, a fire in one of the mine shafts spilled smoke, flames, and poison gas through the tunnels. Many miners died in the panic to get out. Rankin took the side of the miners. She argued unsuccessfully for the government to take the mines out of company hands and to improve conditions. As a result, the Montana legislature, which was dominated by Anaconda, divided the state into separate congressional districts. That made Rankin's district overwhelmingly Democratic. Even if she could overcome her vote against the war, she surely had little chance of reelection now.

As she worked for the causes she believed in, Rankin did not forget her original fight some years earlier. The United States still had not granted suffrage to its female citizens. Decades had passed, and the fight still raged. But now it was 1918. Both political parties finally seemed committed to the cause. In January of that year, Rankin introduced the Anthony Amendment into the House of Representatives. Named in honor of Susan B. Anthony, fighter for the suffragist cause, the amendment would give all American women the right to vote. Senator A. A. Sargent of California had introduced the amendment in 1878. In its original form it called for revising the Fifteenth Amendment of 1870, which states that a person can't be denied the vote because of skin color, race, or a previous condition of slavery.

Rankin gave an impassioned speech to her colleagues in Congress. She spoke of how women had aided the war effort even though they hated war. She asked why women were allowed and encouraged to fight for democracy but were denied the right to participate in it. She asked, "How shall we explain . . . the meaning of democracy if the same Congress that voted for war to make the world safe for democracy refuses to give this small measure of democracy to the women of our country?"

BUTTE: AN ENVIRONMENTAL ISSUE

After the 1917 fire, copper production at the Butte mines steadily declined. In 1955, the largest open-pit copper mine in the United States opened in Butte. Other open-pit mines opened in the area as well. Most of the mining has since stopped, but Butte's environment remains sensitive. Tap water was unsafe to drink for a time in the 1990s. People have found heavy metals such as lead in some former mining areas. Butte may no longer be a notorious mining town of the Old West, but many of the boomtown buildings are still standing and still drawing tourists.

Rankin's speech was followed by a five-hour, heated argument. Opponents had all sorts of reasons to vote no. One claimed that the behavior of the women on the picket line demonstrating for a yes vote was unladylike. Another said that husbands already represented their wives, and this new law would create dissension in the home.

Finally all the arguments were in, and the debate was over. Finally it was time for the roll call. And finally the work of Jeannette Rankin, and of many other dedicated men and women across the country, ended in victory. The amendment passed in the House of Representatives by a vote of 304 to 89.

The Senate vote came two weeks later. On June 5, 1919, after Rankin had left Congress, the Senate joined the House in passing the amendment. The vote was 56 to 25. Next, two-thirds of the state

Rankin delivers her first speech as a member of the House of Representatives.

legislatures had to ratify the amendment. In 1920, the two-thirds mark passed when Tennessee became the thirty-sixth ratifying state. The Nineteenth Amendment was law. The amendment reads as follows: "The right of citizens of the United States to vote shall not be denied or abridged by the United States or any state on account of sex." (Ratified August 18, 1920).

With thanks to Jeannette Rankin and the many men and thousands of women who walked and talked and fought for the cause, any qualified American citizen—male or female—could now vote. They did so in the election of 1921.

CHAPTER FOUR

Time and Dedication

J EANNETTE RANKIN WAS OUT OF A JOB. She could not win a second term in the House. She ran for nomination to the Senate, only to lose there, too. She tried for a third party bid and got 20 percent of the vote. It was a disappointment, but Jeannette Rankin was not a woman easily discouraged. The job was lost, but the cause had yet to be won. So, instead of packing her bags and going to Montana, in May 1919, she went to Zurich, Switzerland.

Four years earlier, Jane Addams and other women advocates for peace had called a conference in Washington, D.C. About three thousand attendees approved a platform including ways to end war. They also established the Women's Peace Party (WPP). In April 1915, their representatives met in The Hague, Netherlands. Included in the agenda was the Second International Conference of Women for Permanent Peace (later the Women's International League for Peace and Freedom), to be convened at the end of World War I. Rankin, along with Jane Addams and other delegates, attended this conference.

THE PEACE CONFERENCE

Headed by Addams, the conference of women in Zurich met at the same time that men were meeting in the vast Versailles Palace near Paris, France. Leaders of the victorious nations were drawing

Portrait of American pacifist leader Jeannette Rankin

up the treaty that would formally end World War I. (The actual fighting ceased with the armistice signed on November 11, 1918.) The timing of the women's conference was no coincidence. Their objective was a just and lasting peace. They wanted a treaty that would make World War I *literally* a war to end all wars. Toward that end, the group drew up a list of recommendations and sent them to President Wilson at Versailles. He said he agreed with their ideas, but to the dismay of the women, the ideas did not become part of the final treaty.

As the women were meeting, the representatives of twenty-one nations were sitting down at the conference table in Versailles. The Big Four were President Wilson of the United States, Prime Minister David Lloyd George of Great Britain, Prime Minister Georges Clemenceau of France, and Prime Minister Vittorio Orlando of Italy. There was trouble almost immediately. Wilson pushed hard for adoption of his Fourteen Points, which he believed were vital to peace. The other three leaders resented what they called Wilson's superior attitude. The conversation got so tense that at one point Wilson had to break up a potential fistfight between Lloyd George and Clemenceau. Orlando walked out of the room for a while, and Wilson threatened to do the same.

The victors at the treaty table in Versailles faced a monumental task. World War I had been long and devastating. The estimated death toll for all nations was 8.5 million, with another 21 million wounded. The fighting had reduced much of northeastern Europe to rubble. Roads, buildings, mines, towns, factories, homes, communication facilities, schools, and hospitals had been destroyed. The victorious countries' leaders were in no mood to be generous and forgiving—and they weren't.

According to the final treaty, Germany had to give up about 13 percent of its territory, about 7 million people, and all its overseas possessions. Alsace-Lorraine, the 5,067 square miles (8,155 square km) that France had ceded to Germany after their war in 1871, was returned. All land taken from Russia was returned as well. The German border areas of Eupen and Malmedy went to Belgium. A region of East Prussia went to Lithuania. Czechoslovakia got the predominantly German-populated Sudetenland. The German army was limited to no more than 100,000 men, the navy could no longer use submarines, and Germany could not have an air force. Germany suffered another severe blow: the loss of the Saar and Upper Silesia regions, which had produced the country's coal. That loss, along with the financial reparations of war, threatened to bankrupt the nation. Germany also had to admit full responsibility for starting the war. German officials signed the treaty under protest. Their choice was to sign the treaty or to suffer an invasion by the Allies.

Rankin and the other delegates at Zurich were very disturbed about the harshness of the Versailles treaty. They were appalled to hear that the defeated countries had not even been invited to sit in

Women at a conference in Zurich protest for peace.

on the conference that decided their fate. Only two obscure German delegates, looking deathly pale, were allowed in. The women asked and discussed some tough questions: Would not such harsh reprisals against the defeated nations only make them more belligerent? Would not belligerent nations be more anxious to return to war? Although some critics derisively called the women "peace-ettes," they could not have been more accurate. As noted in *Primary Documents: Treaty of Versailles*, "Controversial even today, it is often regarded that the punitive terms of the treaty supported the rise of the Nazis and the Third Reich in 1930s Germany, which in turn led to the outbreak of World War II."

When the terms of the Versailles treaty became public, the women at the Zurich conference passed a number of resolutions. They also pointed out sections of the treaty that were dangers to a lasting peace. For instance, the reparations that Germany was required to pay totaled a staggering 226 billion Reichsmarks in gold. That was an impossible amount to pay. To this day, Germany has still not finished paying off its World War I reparations. In addition, there were tight restrictions on manufacturing and the loss of land and colonies. Punitive measures such as these led to massive inflation and a long depression in Germany. When Adolf Hitler appeared in the 1930s, Germans were eager to gain a new pride in themselves. Eventually, the restored pride led to aggression and to World War II.

NEVER WITHOUT WORK

Disappointed about what had not been done, Rankin returned from Europe. She was more and more determined that peace was the only salvation for the world. If she could not work directly for peace, however, she could plunge herself into areas that would make life better for

THE NATIONAL CONSUMERS LEAGUE

The National Consumers League was organized to promote better conditions for workers. Its members pushed for shorter working hours, minimum wages, payment for overtime, and an end to child labor. The league started in England in 1890, and the U.S. group began nine years later under the leadership of Florence Kelley (1859–1932). A social reformer from Philadelphia, Kelley is especially known for her fight for children's rights.

children and the working class. For a time, she worked for the National Consumers League, founded in 1899. She became a lobbyist, urging the government to pass laws to protect workers on their jobs. She argued for laws against employing children in mines and other dangerous workplaces. Working for the National Council for the Prevention of War, she fought for a constitutional amendment that would outlaw going to war. She urged Congress to join the World Court, formally known as the Permanent Court of International Justice, which was established in 1920 by the League of Nations. The idea was for nations to settle their disputes in the courtroom rather than on the battlefield.

The long hours Jeannette Rankin spent for these causes did not always end in success, but many eventually did lead to victories. The eight-hour work day, for instance, became law in 1938, and the five-day work week law passed in the 1940s. In 1938, Congress passed the Fair Labor Standards Act. The law set up a guaranteed minimum wage for workers and time and a half for overtime in certain jobs. Rankin was especially satisfied that the law also stopped most employment of minors in what was called oppressive child labor.

During this period, Rankin spent time at Hull House in Chicago when she was not busy with other causes. She returned to Montana during most summers. She also took time off to work for her brother's campaign for the U.S. Senate. Wellington had lost the Republican bid in 1922 and, despite his sister's help, he lost it again in 1924. He did, however, accept a seat as associate justice of the Montana Supreme Court.

NEW PLACE, SAME CAUSE

Jeannette Rankin turned forty-four in 1924. Against the usual practice of the day, she had little time for or thought of marriage, perhaps because she was so utterly caught up in her causes.

Rankin always remained close to her brother, even though their lives were very different. Wellington devoted himself to making money, which he did in abundance. Rankin, on the other hand, had little interest in making money, and she never became very wealthy. Wellington was supportive of her political ambitions, and he played a large role in her congressional campaigns, even though they strongly disagreed on the subject of war.

Also in 1924, Rankin surprised most of her friends by buying land in north-central Georgia. Recently she had been thinking of a getaway place of her own. Although she was in Montana for summers and holidays, she lived with her brother or one of her sisters at those times. She would always love Montana, but it really was not home anymore, even though it remained her legal residence. Her travels had taken her to rural Georgia, and she liked the quiet, simple atmosphere of the countryside. A far cry from the bustle of Washington, D.C., this area of Georgia was only a day's train ride away, as compared to the four-day trip to and from Montana.

So, Rankin bought 64 acres (26 hectares) of land in Bogart, near Athens, home of the first state-chartered university—the University of Georgia, established in 1785. She built a one-room house with a fireplace but no electricity. There was a well plus a hand pump, but she had no running water inside. Most of her friends did not understand how she could enjoy such conditions. But she did enjoy it, although she admitted it got a little lonely at times. Rankin's mother lived with her, however, and her sisters visited frequently as well. In time, she got to know her neighbors, most of whom where conservative Christians and African Americans with whom she had had little contact previously. It was a kind of life entirely different from what she had known.

Rankin did entertain her suffragette friends from New York and Washington when they could be persuaded to leave their busy cities. But one of her favorite guests was her old friend Fiorello LaGuardia.

Rankin in front of her rural Georgia home

They had met in Washington when both were first-time legislators. At first glance it seemed odd that they would be close friends. Rankin was quiet and reserved, while LaGuardia was loud and boisterous. But he made several trips to see her in Georgia, and they would meet for dinner whenever she was in New York City. Supposedly, Rankin once admitted that LaGuardia had proposed to her. Whether or not that is true, he married his secretary in 1929 and became New York City's best-known, if not best-loved, mayor from 1934 to 1945. He was called the Little Flower, likely a translation of his last name but also because he was short—5 feet 2 inches (1.5 meters). One of New York's major airports is named for him.

She may have been living in a one-room home in out-of-the-way rural Georgia, but that did not keep Rankin from working for peace. She backed a plan proposed by Salmon O. Levinson, a Chicago lawyer who had one of many ideas for outlawing war during this period. Rankin commented, "Instead of having laws about war, we should have laws against war."

She became a lobbyist for the Women's International League for Peace and Freedom (WILPF) and spoke at its fourth congress in Washington, D.C., in 1924. The WILPF wanted their highly effective speaker to be everywhere, and Rankin's schedule became exhausting. She traveled north, south, east, and west across the country in two-week periods. Finally, she decided she could be more effective elsewhere.

Rankin went back to rural Georgia. With some members of the University of Georgia faculty, she founded the Georgia Peace Society in the early 1930s. The cause was the same: get rid of war. Lobbying for the Women's Peace Union, she urged for a constitutional amendment outlawing war. The group drummed home its message by handing out material at state fairs and holding antiwar conferences. The people of rural Georgia tolerated the Women's Peace Union and its activities fairly well until they caught wind of a rumor that the university was establishing a Chair of Peace with Rankin as the first holder. The rumor was not true, but it caused much animosity.

After that, newspapers intimated that Jeannette Rankin was a communist. Infuriated, she filed a lawsuit against a newspaper in Macon. The lawsuit stopped short of a trial when the newspaper published a statement saying she was not a communist. As Rankin said, they declared instead that she was a nice lady, which she found somewhat amusing. The tempest died down, but Rankin later said it was one of the worst experiences of her life.

During the 1930s, Jeannette Rankin continued to preach against war and against abuses to children and workers. In 1938, she went before Congress to testify in support of an amendment introduced by Louis Ludlow, Democrat from Indiana. The law would require a national referendum on any war declaration by Congress, except in cases where the United States was attacked first. Opposed by President Franklin Roosevelt, the amendment was defeated narrowly.

This was only one of many actions by Roosevelt that drew Rankin's intense dislike for the chief executive. She felt his continued election meant more war and more deaths. This anti-Roosevelt feeling persisted throughout her adult life. Roosevelt had voted against suffrage when he was a New York State legislator. He had remarked that women's suffrage might work in the West but certainly not in the eastern states. Rankin never forgave him on that score. Nor did she forgive the women who voted for Roosevelt when he was elected for the last time in 1944. (Roosevelt died in office during his fourth term in 1945.) And, above all, he had voted for war. That was enough for her.

Like many Americans during this period, Rankin watched in quiet horror as a menace began to threaten in Europe once again. As the threat grew closer, a new idea was beginning to take form.

CHAPTER FIVE

Taking a Stand

JEANNETTE RANKIN HAD SPENT ALL OF HER ADULT life fighting against what she saw as the evils of war. Now the threat once again seemed all too real.

Franklin Delano Roosevelt was elected president of the United States in 1933. Adolf Hitler was sworn in as chancellor of Germany in the same year. Following the stock market crash of 1929, the United States suffered a severe economic depression. So did most of Europe. Especially in fledgling democracies, people desperately looked to their leaders for help. Hitler emerged as the answer to Germany's problems. In an incredibly short time, he brought Fascism and Nazism to the country. Fascism is a political doctrine that puts the state above all else. Individual freedom does not exist. Nazism is Fascism with an added element: racial discrimination. According to the Nazi doctrine Hitler adopted, Germans belonged to the Aryan, or Master, race. All other races—meaning inferior ones—were meant to be mastered. At the very bottom of Hitler's inferior list were the Jews.

Rumors about Nazi atrocities against Jews and other minorities soon filtered across the Atlantic. Along with many pacifists, Rankin met with President Roosevelt in Washington. The peacekeepers urged the president to change U.S. immigration laws to admit the Nazis' victims. But the horror continued.

An elderly Rankin once more takes a stand against war.

Prisoners in a World War II German concentration camp

In 1939, while the world watched and did little else, Hitler sent his troops into Austria, and the unchecked march was on. But when the Germans invaded Poland on September 1, Great Britain and France declared war. That did not stop the Nazi killing machine. With lightning speed, it marched through northern Europe.

Now it was 1940. Rankin grew sick with the horror of what was happening in Europe. She was frightened that the United States might become involved again. What could she do to stop it? The answer seemed obvious; why not go back to Congress? Rankin was now sixty years old and in good health. She had been out of government for twenty-three years. Would anyone believe her? Would anyone vote for her?

The answers turned out to be yes and yes. Energetic and as forceful as ever, she ran for Congress on a peace platform. She lectured, talked, and pleaded—at labor meetings, business meetings, church meetings—to anyone who would listen. Her message was always about peace. She promised the people of Montana, as she had years earlier, that she would work to keep their sons from going to war. "Peace is not a job for Santa Claus," she told the crowds, "but for hardworking statesmen. It is not a job for indulgent parents, but for true educators. It is not a job for clever politicians but for international engineers. It is not a job for aged cynics but for hopeful, virile men. And, most important of all, it is not a job for men alone, but preeminently a job for men and women working together."

Just as they had twenty-three years earlier, Montana voters listened to the lady from Missoula. On election day, she received 90,000 more votes than did her opponent. And, in March 1941, Jeannette Rankin was back in Congress. The woman had returned to the House. But the atmosphere was different; this time she wasn't alone. Five other women now sat in the House of Representatives, and two were in the Senate. Now that she was no longer the only female in government, Rankin remarked that no one would pay any attention to her. It did not exactly work out that way.

THE THREAT GROWS CLOSER

By June 1940, the Nazi powers occupied three-fifths of France, including Paris. Only the Royal Air Force kept the British Isles safe for the time being. There seemed no end to the massive German war machine; Hungary, Romania, Bulgaria, Yugoslavia, and Greece soon fell. And in June 1941, Hitler launched an attack against the Soviet Union.

ATTACK ON PEARL HARBOR

The surprise was total. In two waves that took perhaps two hours, Japanese planes dealt a staggering blow to the American military force stationed at Pearl Harbor, Hawaii, on December 7, 1941. The first wave of planes hit at 7:53 a.m., the second at 8:55.

By early afternoon, the carriers that had launched the aircraft were headed back to Japan.

The destruction was stunning. Thousands died, and hundreds of planes and other military facilities were destroyed or crippled. But most importantly for U.S. war efforts, the fuel oil storage facilities had not been touched. This helped to get the American military machine running again. That ultimately led to the Battle of Midway in June 1942, when U.S. forces defeated a Japanese invasion, and to the end of the Japanese empire in 1948.

In the meantime, on the other side of the world, Japan was growing tired of its long, indecisive war with China. Japanese troops began to seize European properties in the Far East. Although the United States was not involved in the fighting, Japan viewed the Americans as a possible threat. On December 7, 1941, the Japanese bombed U.S. naval installations at Pearl Harbor, Hawaii, in a surprise attack. The next day, the United States was at war with all the Axis powers.

After her first election to Congress, Jeannette Rankin was involved in voting yes or no for war. After the bombing of Pearl Harbor, she was once more faced with the same decision.

The speech that President Roosevelt gave to Congress on the morning of December 8, 1941, came as no surprise to the legislators. Nor were there any surprises about his last few remarks:

> I believe I interpret the will of the Congress and of the people when I assert that we will not only defend ourselves to the uttermost but will make very certain that this form of treachery shall never happen again. . . .
>
> I ask that the Congress declare that since the unprovoked and dastardly attack by Japan on Sunday, December seventh, a state of war has existed between the United States and the Japanese Empire.

Now it was up to Congress to vote for war.

THE SECOND VOTE

Rankin was in Pittsburgh, Pennsylvania, on her way to a speaking engagement when she heard that Congress would take up the war vote on Monday. She hurried back to Washington but talked to no one about her vote. As she later recalled, "I did not want to talk with anyone. I was much more upset than I had been in 1917. Then I had been sad. But this time I was grieved at seeing the men who were as opposed to going into the war as I was slipping away from their position at the critical moment."

As she had years earlier, Rankin thought long and hard about her decision. In the end, the result was the same. When the roll call came, once more she voted no.

> ## As a woman I cannot go to war, and I refuse to send anyone else.

It was the second time that Jeannette Rankin voted against U.S. entry into a war. She had been vilified for her vote against World War I. This time, the public reaction was worse. This time, she was the lone dissenting vote against an action that almost all Americans felt morally justified in pursuing. American people and American soil had been attacked. A mad and determined killer was systematically wiping out people on the other side of the Atlantic. Evil had a face. U.S. citizens were angry, and they showed their anger to the woman from Montana.

The United States formally declared war on Germany and the Axis powers on December 8. Three days later, the Axis declared war on the United States. World War II was about to engulf nearly all the world.

Immediately after Rankin's vote, the House chamber erupted into shouts of rage. When she walked out of the chamber, an angry mob nearly attacked her. She closed herself in a phone booth, where police rescued her and took her to her office. She soon received a telegram from Wellington, who said the whole state was against her. Other telegrams were not so nice. Even her old suffragette friends were angry. They said she had disgraced them.

Not everyone was against her, however. Although he disagreed with her decision, her friend Fiorello LaGuardia said he admired Rankin for standing by her convictions. The American Civil Liberties Union sided with her vote, as did many others for the pacifist cause.

The severe reaction against her no vote to war in 1941 sent Rankin into a telephone booth for safety.

THE WORLD AT WAR

Even if Rankin had not been the target of such rage, she would have had little chance to work for peace in Congress. The entire government, as well as the entire country, was preoccupied with war. And although the power of the U.S. military machine promised a victory, it was long and hard in coming.

In early 1942, the first American forces arrived in Great Britain. By June, the mass murder of Jews by gassing began at Auschwitz, one of the Nazi death camps. The war would drag on for three more years.

FREE SPEECH

If an American opposes an existing social condition, such as racism or sexism, he or she can openly criticize the government. The First Amendment to the U.S. Constitution protects this right, which is known as freedom of speech. There are conditions attached to this freedom, however. For instance, it is illegal to make speeches that incite violence or advocate child pornography. But even with these restrictions, the protections of the First Amendment are regarded as some of the broadest of any industrialized nation.

As the nation remained engrossed in the machinery of war, Rankin waited out the rest of her term with little to do. The causes she normally advocated were pushed into the background. Condemned by the press and avoided by many of her colleagues, she tried to cut herself off from public exposure. She said later that she often drove around Washington instead of walking so that she would not have to meet with people. She refused to take the X gasoline ration card, which gave extra gas to members of Congress. And she found solace in old friends such as LaGuardia, who was often in Washington on civil defense business.

At last, by early 1945, victory seemed to be in sight. Soviet troops entered the German capital of Berlin in April. Knowing the end was near, a crazed Hitler committed suicide on April 30. Victory was declared in Europe on May 8, but the fight continued in Japan.

In July, the United States tested the world's first atomic bomb. On August 6, the Americans dropped their bomb on Hiroshima, Japan. The Japanese did not surrender. A second U.S. bomb hit Nagasaki on August 9. Japan surrendered on August 14. V-J (Victory over Japan) Day was declared on September 2, 1945. In October, the United Nations was born. On November 20, the Nuremberg war trials against the Axis powers began.

" And *now* what? Did we win the war? Did we settle anything? Did we bring a lasting peace? The war to put down 'Prussian militarism' ushered in an era of armed truce, with growing tension between nations as the preparations for another war have steadily increased. . . . All of which proves that the last war was a magnificent dud, and indicates that the next one will, along with wiping out civilization, prove somewhat disappointing to those who follow the will-o-the-wisp of using war for idealistic purposes. The last 'war to end war' should have taught us that we can't end war that way. Wars pave the way for more war. **"**

ON THE WAY OUT AGAIN

For the second time, Jeannette Rankin's political career was ruined. People continued to write letters attacking her. A letter from the Republican National Committee in Montana told her to change her vote.

Rankin could only reply that she had to vote her conscience. The *New York Times* said her judgment could not be trusted. One Presbyterian cleric suggested that she resign. Even with the help of friends and a few like-minded strangers, this was a time of great strain for Jeannette Rankin. With so many against her, her position in the House seemed useless. What could she do in Washington for the rest of her term?

Rankin was never a woman to be idle. She worked to secure war contracts for small businesses around the country. She tried—unsuccessfully—to pass laws aimed at reducing the possibility of war: no money granted by Congress for foreign wars; no arming of civilian ships; a public vote before a military draft could be started; a public referendum before Congress could vote to declare war; and no death penalty for sabotage during wartime.

When the long year was over, Rankin took comfort in returning to both Georgia and Montana. During her second term in office, her home in Georgia had burned down. She experimented with building a new, inexpensive house of packed earth. She abandoned the project halfway through, however. In 1945, she moved into a former sharecropper's three-room cabin instead. She paid $500 for the house and 30 acres (12 hectares) of land. She named her new home Shady Grove. This time she had electricity, but it would be another twenty years before there was running water.

Rankin's family often said she liked to appear poor, especially in Georgia, as a protest against American commercial values. But the choice was not about appearances. Although she did not have a lot of money, her property in Georgia became quite valuable over the years. Whenever she needed to, she could sell off parcels of land.

Each summer, as she had practically all her adult life, Rankin packed up and went to Montana. For some time, she had driven a car there instead of taking the train. Her car was one of her few luxuries, even though it was often a second-hand jalopy.

In Montana, Rankin stayed at Wellington's ranch, where her mother had lived since becoming ill in Washington in 1941. Olive, now old, cranky, and obese, required a series of nurses to care for her.

No matter where she was, Jeannette Rankin never lost her interest in politics or her rage against war. But in the years following her second term in Congress, she largely disappeared from public view. Much of that time, she traveled. Occasionally she would sell a few acres of her land in Georgia to finance a trip. And Wellington continued to be generous with money.

In 1946, with the war over, Rankin decided to take a six-month world tour. One of the places she most wanted to visit was India. She especially admired Mahatma Gandhi, India's spiritual leader, and his nonviolent campaign for his country's independence. Gandhi had brought down a mighty empire through his power of passive resistance. This was totally in tune with Rankin's beliefs.

Rankin also had read the work of American author Henry David Thoreau, including his essay "Civil Disobedience" (1849). Over time, she came to believe that both Gandhi and Thoreau had discovered how people could avoid war. Earlier, she had thought that it was right for the United States to arm for defense purposes only. Now she felt that total universal disarmament was the only answer. If a gun was handy, she believed, men would find a way to use it.

On her visit to India, Rankin met with Jawaharlal Nehru, who became India's first prime minister when the country gained independence in 1947. Rankin very much wanted to meet Gandhi on this trip. However, the spiritual leader was caught up in trying to stop the bloody war between Hindus and Muslims.

Rankin made numerous trips to India. She never met Gandhi,

THE GREAT SOUL

Mohandas Karamchand Gandhi (1869–1948), considered the father of India, was the leader of the nationalist movement to rid his nation of British rule. Gandhi is known internationally for his doctrine of nonviolent protest to achieve social progress.

In 1857, Indian troops, called sepoys, unsuccessfully rebelled against the British East India Company, a trading monopoly. The following year, Great Britain took over rule of India. Gandhi went to study in England in 1888 and was shocked at the racial discrimination he found there. Upon his return to India, he entered politics and became the head of the Indian National Congress. He vowed to achieve Indian independence without violence. He led freedom marches and went on hunger strikes to protest British rule. The British called his methods unlawful. Gandhi was imprisoned for so-called civil disobedience throughout much of World War II. But largely through his efforts, India achieved independence in August 1947. Gandhi was killed by a Hindu fanatic the following January.

Rankin admired Indian leader Mohandas Gandhi, shown here as he sits cross-legged on the floor of his home.

however, because he was assassinated before her second trip in 1949. She attended a world peace conference there and even took her car—a Ford this time—along. After the conference, she hired a driver and toured the country. In 1952, she spent a year in the northern mountains of India. She also traveled to South Africa, Europe, and South America.

Confident and friendly, Rankin never seemed to mind traveling alone. There was always someone nearby to chat with the smiling, white-haired woman from Missoula.

CHAPTER SIX

The Aim Is Peace

R ANKIN ALWAYS RETURNED FROM HER TRAVELS to India and Europe with the scars of World War II planted firmly in her mind. But in the 1950s, she had a new concern. The United States was involved in another military conflict. This time it was Korea.

For centuries, China and Japan had fought over the small Korean peninsula in East Asia. Finally, in 1910, after war with China, Japan took control of the peninsula. But when Japan lost World War II, part of its surrender terms included the loss of Korea. The peninsula was divided into North Korea, under Soviet control, and South Korea, occupied by U.S. forces. The dividing line was the thirty-eighth parallel. Soviet troops withdrew in 1948, and the U.S. military left the following year.

On June 25, 1950, North Koreans crossed the thirty-eighth parallel. Two days later, President Harry Truman authorized American forces to defend South Korea. The United Nations pledged fifteen other countries to join the United States. Due to U.S. and Soviet Union involvement, the conflict became an enlargement of the so-called Cold War between the superpowers.

The fighting lasted until July 27, 1953. An estimated 3 million people died, including more than 54,000 Americans. The war played a large role in the election of Dwight D. Eisenhower as U.S. president in 1952. The former general had pledged to end the war and go to Korea if elected—and he did.

Rankin at Avalanche Ranch, about 1952

The Korean War was the first armed conflict of the Cold War. As such, it set new patterns for later disagreements. One of these new patterns was called limited warfare. The two superpowers could now fight each other in a third country, while the third country suffered most of the war damages. And, indeed, both Koreas suffered heavily. Today, a heavily guarded demilitarized zone (the DMZ) on the thirty-eighth parallel still divides the peninsula. No formal peace treaty has ended the war.

The fighting in Korea confirmed Rankin's fears that the world would never change. She once said, "So long as we want war, or are resigned to war, we shall have it. Weapons will be found."

THE MARCH AGAINST WAR

In the 1960s, American citizens became increasingly unhappy about the nation's involvement with war. By that time, the United States was involved in a new Cold War conflict—war in Vietnam, Laos, and Cambodia—which would not end until 1975. The 1960s were also a time of domestic restlessness and conflict, such as nonviolent protests against racial discrimination. In 1955, Martin Luther King Jr. (1929–1968), an African-American clergyman and leader in the U.S. civil rights movement, had led the Montgomery (Alabama) bus boycott that desegregated the city's buses. In March 1963, he led the March on Washington for Jobs and Freedom. About 250,000 marchers—black and white—demanded civil rights laws and an end to racial discrimination. It was the largest gathering of protesters in the nation's capital to that time.

In his "I Have a Dream" speech on that day, King outlined his hopes for his children and his country. Along with Abraham Lincoln's Gettysburg Address and Franklin Roosevelt's Infamy Speech, King's speech is regarded as one of the finest in American history.

Five years after King's huge demonstration for civil rights, there was another march on Washington. Nearly five thousand women crowded the streets of the capital on the opening day of Congress, January 15, 1968. They were a coalition of women's groups united for a specific purpose. This time they marched for peace. Their goal was to present a strong show of female opposition to the war on the other side of the world in Vietnam.

On that snowy January day, the women were led by a longtime antiwar disciple and the oldest living suffrage fighter. Jeannette Rankin was now eighty-seven years old. She had come to Washington to join her much younger war protesters. They called themselves the Jeannette Rankin Brigade.

Dr. Martin Luther King Jr., second from the right, waves during a five-day march from Selma to Montgomery, Alabama, in 1965.

Members of the Women's Brigade, led by Rankin, protest the Vietnam War in Washington, D.C., January 15, 1968.

It was a remarkable sight. Clad in black, the group of women, which included King's widow, Coretta, met at Union Station that morning in the nation's capital. With Rankin walking briskly in front, they marched to Union Square across from the Capitol. There they held a peaceful rally, but police arrested a few protesters when they tried to walk on the grounds of the Capitol. Most of the marchers were white and middle-aged. Many women viewed the brigade as a focal point in the cause of liberation for women. A few hundred of the younger marchers felt the demonstration was without "teeth," however. They tried unsuccessfully to stir up trouble to get Congress to do something to end the war.

The marchers felt it unfair that, by city statute, they could not walk, stand, or demonstrate on the grounds of the Capitol. So, they decided to sue. In *Jeannette Rankin Brigade v. Capitol Police*, the women charged that their First Amendment rights had been violated. The First Amendment states in part that Congress cannot make a law that prohibits "the right of the people peaceably to assemble." Later on, in 1971, police used the same statute to arrest 990 marchers who had gathered on the Capitol steps to hear antiwar speeches by several members of Congress.

A three-judge district court decided the *Brigade* case in May 1972. The women won. The court said the statute was unconstitutional and declared that First Amendment freedoms need space to exist. The government appealed the decision, but the U.S. Supreme Court upheld it on November 6, 1972.

THE MARCH AGAINST WAR

The Jeannette Rankin Brigade was protesting the war in Vietnam when its members marched on Washington. The war that began in 1959 was fought between communist North Vietnam and its allies and South Vietnam, which was supported by the United States and other allies.

The combatants signed a peace treaty in 1973, but the fighting continued. Then the U.S. Congress prohibited further intervention by American troops. The last U.S. Marines pulled out on April 30. North and South Vietnam were unified the following year.

The communists attained their goal of reuniting Vietnam, but it was a costly war on all sides. Some 3 to 4 million North and South Vietnamese died, as well as more than 58,000 American troops. To many, the fighting in Vietnam was proof that not even a superpower had unlimited resources and strength. Said a heartsick Jeannette Rankin before the end of the fighting,

> **I would like to think I did my job well [referring to her terms in Congress], in good conscience, and with whole-hearted devotion to the welfare of my country.**
>
> **It is the same conscience and devotion which compel me now, at age eighty-six, to oppose with all my heart and strength this illegal and terrible war in Vietnam.**
>
> **I could be told that I am an old woman; that this is no longer my time nor my world and to leave the business of the fighting and the dying to those with the years for living. But I cannot now, nor could I at any age, deny life.**

The war in Vietnam put Rankin back in the public eye and back in newspaper headlines. Once again, she began making protest speeches. She especially called out for women to resist the fighting. She was adamant in her belief that women could and should have a stronger voice in military affairs.

Her timing could not have been better. Long an antiwar advocate, she now was part of the most successful antiwar movement in U.S. history. As Americans became frustrated with the endless fighting in Vietnam, protests grew larger and more strident. Polite, conservatively dressed protesters were replaced by people who were labeled hippies because of their long hair and casual dress. Protest music by artists such as Bob Dylan and Joan Baez filled the air. This new counterculture, along with time-tested antiwar advocates such as Jeannette Rankin, played an important role in restraining U.S. war

WHAT HAPPENED TO THE RANKIN CLAN?

Edna (sister): The sixth child born to the Rankins, she attended Wellesley College and the University of Wisconsin. She graduated with a law degree from the University of Montana.

Grace (sister): The seventh and last child, she graduated from the University of Montana and spent most of her life caring for her mother.

Harriet (sister): The third child, she worked for fourteen years at the University of Montana, part of the time as dean of women.

John (father): He contracted Rocky Mountain spotted fever, an infection usually caused by a wood tick or dog tick, and died in 1904.

Mary (sister): The fifth child, she earned degrees from Wellesley College and the University of Montana. She taught English at the University of Montana as well as in high schools in California.

Olive (mother): After her husband's death, her obesity led to greater health problems. She died in Montana in 1947.

Philena (sister): The second child born to the Rankins, she died in early childhood.

Wellington (brother): He married twice. The second time was in 1956, when he was seventy-two years old. He died at the Mayo Clinic in 1966 after abdominal surgery.

efforts—including a hastening of troop withdrawals under Presidents Lyndon Johnson and Richard Nixon.

RETIREMENT

The Jeanette Rankin Brigade march and other protest speeches rekindled an old idea in the minds of many Americans: Rankin should run for a third term in Congress. But this time she declined. Health problems were slowing her down. She walked with a cane due to a broken hip, and an operation for a painful nerve had caused the left side of her face and her eyelid to droop. She had lost much of her hair and now wore a wig. Although her mind was still active and she was still passionate about the cause for peace, her body had become quite frail. Almost against her own will, she bought a retirement home in Carmel, California, near where her sister Edna lived.

But *retirement* was not really a word in Rankin's vocabulary. With her revived popularity after the march, many people offered her speaking engagements—and she accepted as long as she was physically able. Peace was always at the top of her agenda. The grand old lady of the antiwar cause kept on protesting as long as she could.

Rankin had other causes besides peace. She saw herself as a representative for women. Early in her career she had fought for women's right to vote. Throughout her life, she had advocated equal pay for women, birth control rights, and child welfare. And at the age of ninety-two, in Washington, D.C., she was given the Susan B. Anthony Award for the living woman who had done the most for women's rights.

When she wasn't campaigning against war, Rankin also had fought—mostly unsuccessfully—for political changes. For example, she was against the Electoral College, a group of popularly elected representatives who formally select the U.S. president and vice president. Rather

Rankin, at age ninety-two, receives the first Susan B. Anthony Award given by the National Organization for Women in New York City, February 12, 1972.

than directly voting for a candidate, U.S. citizens cast votes for electors. The electors pledge to vote for specific candidates, but technically they can vote for anyone who is eligible. Rankin felt this system restricts voters' choices. She was also against winner-take-all congressional districts. She felt they favored the better-known male candidates.

In HER WILL

In her will, Jeannette Rankin left her property in Georgia to unemployed women workers. Several women used $16,000 from the estate to create the Jeannette Rankin Foundation, based in Athens, Georgia. The foundation offers scholarships to working women, aged thirty-five and older, who need help with undergraduate or vocational programs. Its first scholarship, awarded in 1978, was for $500 and was given to a nursing student. In 2007, the organization offered eighty scholarships of $2,000 each.

Rankin had many ideas about social issues as well. Some of those ideas were quite unusual for the time and angered many people. For instance, she felt that newspapers should change the way they shape public opinion. She wanted the government to own newspapers and run them much the same way as public schools were run. In Rankin's view, newspapers should be free. And they should carry only the news, without editorial opinion. These notions did not make her a friend of many newspapers throughout the country.

Rankin was also interested in the idea of collective living. In 1966, she decided to build a commune on her Georgia property. Designed for older woman, this circular home—what she called a round house—had a central living area surrounded by ten small bedrooms, each with a half bath. The round house also had one full bath and shower, a community kitchen, and lots of room for gardening. She planned to charge a rent of fifteen dollars a month, and she envisioned the ten women living like a family.

The problem was that nobody came. One disadvantage was that the round house was unfurnished. Another drawback might have been its location in rural Georgia, which, as Rankin had to admit, was not to everyone's taste. Also, in the matter of taste, she was a somewhat unusual dresser. Many of her first-time visitors were shocked to discover how she lived in rural Georgia. Her lifestyle was modest to say the least. Never one to fuss about her clothing, she might spend the entire day in her bathrobe. More times than not, she looked as though she was wearing something that she had just picked up off the floor. She had often angered her mother by taking something a sister or relative had thrown away and wearing it around the ranch. She said that she just wanted to be comfortable—and that there were many Americans who couldn't afford to dress any better than she did.

Yet, Rankin always looked proper in public or in the chambers of Congress, even though her outfits might have been different from most. For instance, in 1961 her old college gave her an honorary law degree. She showed up for the occasion in a silk dress, with her gray hair highlighted with red streaks. In 1968, at an interview, she wore high black boots and a Shirley Temple wig. In 1972, she wore a Shanghai silk dress to a TV interview with David Frost. It seemed she had bought the dress just for that occasion. After the interview, she told an aide to take it back to the store.

Even as her body grew frail, Rankin's mind never slowed down. Nor did her passion for her causes. But, finally, even for this confirmed advocate, there came a time. The last march was marched, the last flag was waved, and the last war was scorned. Jeannette Rankin of Missoula, Montana, two-time member of Congress, an uncompromising woman of principle, died in her sleep in Carmel, California, on May 18, 1973. She was nearly ninety-three years old.

CHAPTER SEVEN

The Rankin Legacy

J EANNETTE RANKIN WAS THE FIRST WOMEN elected to the U.S. Congress. But her election went beyond just that history-making fact. She broke all gender barriers with her election. She was a pacifist—a person who opposes war, often under any circumstances, as a way to settle disputes. Many people are against war in theory. But many will accept it under certain circumstances, such as fighting an enemy who made the first attack. But Jeannette Rankin was not a pacifist in theory. She lived it. Both times, she knew what her no vote would mean to her career in Congress. Both times, she voted with her conscience. She said no to war because she believed that war, under any circumstances, is wrong.

Rankin probably knew that her no votes would not stop war and might well ruin her career. But perhaps she thought her votes would give people the strength to vote their conscience in the future. Always true to her convictions, she later said that she never regretted either of her no votes in Congress. She declared that if she had it to do over, she would do the same thing. And indeed, for the rest of her life, she never seemed to regret her actions.

Rankin on her no vote in 1917: "As the first woman to sit in the legislature of any sovereign nation, I cast my first vote in April 1917 against the entry of the United States into World War I. As I said at the time, I wanted to stand by my country, but I could not vote for war. I look back with satisfaction on that momentous occasion."

Statues of pacifist Jeannette Rankin (1880-1973) and astronaut John L. Swigert Jr. (1931-1982) on display at Emancipation Hall, Washington, D.C., in the newly finished Capitol Visitor Center on Capitol Hill, November 10, 2008

On her no vote in 1941: "This time I stood alone. It was a good deal more difficult than it had been the time before. Yet I think the men in Congress all sensed that I would note 'No' again. If I had done otherwise, I do not think I could have faced the remaining days of Congress. Even the men who were most convinced that we had to get into the war would have lost respect for me if I had betrayed my convictions."

Jeannette Rankin was a crusader for the rights of women—the right to vote and the end to discrimination on the basis of gender. But she was often critical of women after they gained the right to vote. She criticized them for not rallying around female candidates and for, in essence, voting just about the same way as men did. She believed that with their votes, women could change humanity's constant march to war through the centuries. Peacemaking, she believed, was a woman's natural role.

Rankin claimed to be pessimistic about the male sex. Her philosophy was simple: men start wars. Perhaps that is why she had a short fuse when it came to judging public figures, since most of them were men. Her dislike of Franklin Roosevelt was long-standing; she thought he was a dictator. She did not like Dwight Eisenhower or Lyndon Johnson because of their participation in war.

Jeannette Rankin was a woman way ahead of her time. She lived in a society that had long rejected the possibility of women in the voting booth, to say nothing of women in Congress. What she saw as the injustices of society and the evils of war shaped her life and her personality. She did not, however, believe that the answers to the problems of society would come from the common man or woman. She wanted everyday citizens on her side, but on her own terms and implementing her own ideas of justice and morality.

Jeannette Rankin ran into many obstacles throughout her lifetime. She fought people who supported war or opposed women's suffrage. She fought those who would ignore the plight of abused children or the working poor. And she also fought herself. She was by nature a reserved woman, but she was also stubborn. She was determined never to let her personal problems interfere with her life's work. And she never did.

Jeannette Rankin has been described in many ways. She has been called the greatest feminist of all time, the most dedicated pacifist, or the most forceful advocate for the rights of women. To some degree those statements might be true. However, the real story of this woman is perhaps not so dramatic but just as admirable. Rankin believed that war is wrong. She believed that injustice is wrong. And no threats to her or to her career could make war or injustice right. That is why she voted no. And that is why Jeannette Rankin should be remembered, above all, as a woman of conscience.

> **If I had my life to live over, I would do it all again. But this time I would be nastier.**

TIMELINE

1880	Born June 11
1898	Graduates from high school
1902	Graduates from the University of Montana; takes trip with friends to West Coast
1904	Teaches school at Grant Creek
1905	Spends six months with a friend and Wellington on the East Coast
1907	Works to help immigrant children on Telegraph Hill, San Francisco
1908–1909	Studies social work in New York City
1909	Returns to Missoula, then to the University of Washington
1910	Works successfully for women's right to vote in Washington State
1911	Becomes social worker in New York City
1914	Works successfully for women's right to vote in Montana
1915	*Lusitania* is sunk, May 7; World War I begins in Europe
1916	Upon election to the House of Representatives, becomes first woman in Congress, November 7

1917	Becomes the only female member of Congress (along with 50 men) to vote no on entering World War I.; United States enters World War I; Butte mine explosion, June 6
1918	Term in Congress ends; Woodrow Wilson delivers Fourteen Points speech; World War I ends, November 11
1919	Nineteenth Amendment grants women's suffrage in the United States; attends women's peace conference in Zurich, May; returns home and works for National Consumers League
1924	Buys property in rural Georgia; lobbies for Women's International League for Peace and Freedom
1930s	Organizes Georgia Peace Society; is falsely accused of being a communist
1935	Home in Georgia burns; moves to new home
1940	Elected again to the House of Representatives, March
1941	Japan attacks Pearl Harbor, December 7; Jeannette is sole member of Congress to vote no on war with Japan, December 8; United States enters World War II
1946	Takes six-month European tour
1949–1952	Travels in Europe, India, and South America
1968	Jeannette Rankin Brigade marches against war in Washington, D.C., January 15
1972	Jeannette is awarded Susan B. Anthony Award
1973	Dies in Carmel, California, at the age of ninety-two, May 18

SOURCE NOTES

Boxed quotes unless otherwise noted

CHAPTER 1

p. 5, par. 4, "Franklin D. Roosevelt's Infamy Speech, "University of Oklahoma College of Law: A Chronology of U.S. Historical Documents, www.law. ou.edu/ushistory/infamy/shtml.

p. 12, par. 1, Norma Smith, *Jeannette Rankin: America's Conscience* (Helena: Montana Historical Society Press, 2002), p. 34.

p. 15, par. 2, James J. Lopach and Jean A. Luckowski, *Jeannette Rankin: A Political Woman* (Boulder: University of Colorado Press, 2005), p. 23.

p. 17, Jeannette Rankin, "'Two Votes against War' and Other Writings on Peace," A.J. Muste Memorial Institute Essay Series No. 14, New York, p. 5 (pamphlet).

p. 18, par. 1, Rankin, "'Two Votes against War,'" p. 5.

CHAPTER 3

p. 35, par. 2, "Jeannette Rankin," http://womenshistory.about.com/od/congress/a/jeanette_rankin.htm.

p. 41, par. 2, "Wilson's War Message to Congress," 2 April 1917, World War I Document Archive, http://wwi.lib.byu.edu/index.php/Wilson%27s_War_Message_to_Congress.

p. 43, "Jeannette Rankin, A Future without War," afww.wordpress.com/2010/06/28.

p. 45, par. 2, Rankin, "Two Votes," p. 27.

CHAPTER 4

p. 52, par. 1, "Primary Documents: Treaty of Versailles, 28 June 1919," www.firstworldwar.com/source/versailles.htm, p. 1.

p. 56, par. 2, Smith, *Jeannette Rankin*, p. 124.

CHAPTER 5

p. 61, par. 1, Rankin, "Two Votes," p. 20.

p. 63, par. 4, Rankin, "Two Votes," p. 11.

p. 64, par. 1, Rankin, "Two Votes," p. 11.

p. 67, par. 2, "Jeannette Rankin: Women's Voices," http://womenshistory.about.com/od/congress/a/jeanette_rankin.htm.

CHAPTER 6

p. 74, par. 1, Rankin, "Two Votes," p. 11.

p. 78, par. 1, Rankin, "Two Votes," p. 38.

CHAPTER 7

p. 85, par. 3, Rankin, "Two Votes," p. 5.

p. 86, par. 1, Rankin, "Two Votes," p. 11.

p. 87, Jana Bommersback, "No Compromise with War," *True West* magazine, 3/1/07, p. 2.

FURTHER INFORMATION

BOOKS

Baker, Jean H. *Sisters: The Lives of America's Suffragists.* New York : Hill & Wang, 2006.

Marx, Trish. *Jeannette Rankin: First Lady of Congress.* New York: MacElderry, 2006.

Rau, Dana Meachen. *Great Women of the Suffrage Movement.* Mankato, MN: Compass Point, 2006.

Ruth, Janice E. and Evelyn Sinclair. *Women Who Dare: Women of the Suffrage Movement.* Petaluma, CA: Pomegranate, 2006.

Woelfle, Gretchen. *Jeannette Rankin: Political Pioneer.* Honesdale, PA: Calkins Creek, 2007.

WEBSITES

The Jeannette Rankin Peace Center
Website of the Jeannette Rankin Peace Center and its work for world peace.
www.jrpc.org

Montana
Official website of the state of Montana.
mt.gov

Official Kids' Portal for the U.S. Government
A challenging, fun look at how the U.S. government works.
www.kids.gov

BIBLIOGRAPHY

BOOKS

Lang, William L. and Rex C. Meyers. *Montana: Our Land and People.* Boulder, CO: Preuett, 1979.

Lopach, James J. and Jean A. Luckowski. *Jeannette Rankin: A Political Woman.* Boulder: University of Colorado Press, 2005.

Smith, Norma. *Jeannette Rankin: America's Conscience.* Helena: Montana Historical Society Press, 2002.

PAMPHLET

Rankin, Jeannette. "'Two Votes Against War' and Other Writings for Peace," A. J. Muste Memorial Institute Essay Series No. 14, 339 Lafayette St., New York.

ARTICLES

Brown, Mackey. "Montana's First Woman Politician." *Montana Business Quarterly*, autumn 1971, 23-26.

Kennedy, John F. "A Woman of Courage." *McCall's*, July 1958, 23-26.

Larson, T. A. "Montana Women and the Battle for the Ballot." *Montana: The Magazine of Western History*, winter 1973, 34.

McNamee, Wally. "The Women March." *Washington Post*, January 16, 1968. 1A.

ABOUT THE AUTHOR

CORINNE J. NADEN is the author of more than 125 books for young readers and adults. A former U.S. Navy journalist and children's book editor, she lives in Tarrytown, New York.